The Resurrection of the Body

I0171128

E W Bullinger

ISBN: 978-1-78364-362-2

The Open Bible Trust
Fordland Mount, Upper Basildon,
Reading, RG8 8LU, UK.

www.obt.org.uk

The Resurrection of the Body

Contents

Page

The Resurrection of the Body 4

Introduction

Introduction

There are few subjects that are made more of in the word of God, and there are few subjects that are more set at nought by the traditions of men, than the doctrine of the Resurrection. I believe that it was the late Mr. Spurgeon who lamented the fact that our English theology, while it was rich in every department of Christian doctrine, does not contain a single satisfactory work upon it; and a reference to a bibliography of the subject, such as you find in Alger's *Future State,* will convince anyone of that fact—a fact as instructive as it is remarkable.

- We are all constantly confessing in our Creed, "I look for the resurrection of the dead". Do we look for it?

- We are all as constantly confessing, "I believe in the forgiveness of sins". Do we believe it?

I think that the two may go together; and we may say of them that all the thousands who take the Christian name upon their lips know little about the forgiveness of sins, and look but little for the resurrection of the dead.

It was with special reference to the resurrection that our blessed Lord said to His enemies, "Ye do err, not knowing the Scriptures, nor the power of God". And we err with regard to this subject of the transformation of His people, because we are ignorant of what the word of God has to say about it; and we are ignorant, upon the other hand, about all that flows from the knowledge of the forgiveness of sin, because we are ignorant of the blessed standing and privilege which He has given us. We separate ourselves from Christ; we separate this great doctrine from Christ;

and hence it is that, while He holds out the blessed hope for troubled hearts, and says, "If I go away, I will come again and receive you unto Myself", and "I am coming to gather My saints, to raise them that are asleep, and to change them and those that are alive and remain", we reply practically, "No, Lord, Thou needs not come for me; I am going to die, and come to Thee".

While we may draw our own inferences from what the Scriptures state, we shall all agree that it is highly important that we should clothe those views in Scriptural terms, and that we should ask and answer how far it is that this popular saying has practically, at any rate until recent years, blotted out the hope of the Lord's coming again to fulfil His promise, to receive us to Himself. And also how far it has practically blotted out the hope of resurrection and disestablished it from the place it occupies in the word of God, and disestablished it altogether from the Church's various hymn-books as a great object of hope.

Resurrection in John 6

Resurrection in John 6

This error crept into the Church at a very early date. You remember how the apostle speaks to some, in the 15th chapter of 1st Corinthians, who say that there is "no resurrection of the dead"; and in writing to Timothy he refers to Hymenaeus and Philetus, who had led away some from the faith by saying that "the resurrection is past already". It is remarkable, and it is instructive and worthy of all attention, that, though there is so little said about death in the New Testament, and nothing about it at any rate as a hope; and though there is so much said about the blessed hope of the transformation of His people at their resurrection, yet in the 6th of John, four times in a few verses, Jesus says,

> "This is the Father's will which hath sent Me, that of all which He hath given Me I should lose nothing, but should *raise it up again at the last day*". (John 6:39)

And again,

> "This is the will of Him that sent Me" (so that the words of Jesus really are the Father's will), "that every one which seeth the Son, and believeth on Him, may have everlasting life"; and, more than that, *"I will raise him up at the last day"*. (John 6:40)

And again,

> "No man can come to Me, except the Father which hath

sent Me draw him: and *I will raise him up at the last day".*
(John 6:44)

And again,

> "Whoso eateth My flesh, and drinketh My blood, hath
> eternal life; and *I will raise him up at the last day"* (John
> 6:54).

The greatest comfort which the greatest Comforter that the world
ever knew had to give for a sister who had been bereaved of a
beloved brother was, "Thy brother shall rise again". All hope is
bound up with this great subject. If our Theology has no place in
it for this great hope, then the sooner we change it the better; for
remember that this subject is one wholly of revelation. There is
not a man on the face of the earth who can tell us anything
whatever about it, except what he himself learns from the word of
God. It is not therefore a question of human reasoning; it is not a
question of the opinion of great or learned men; it is not a
question of any system of doctrine or of philosophy; but it is
purely a question of Divine revelation.

Our eyes see at every street corner at the present moment a
placard advertising a book, *Death and afterwards,* by a poor
mortal woman; and what can she tell us about it? What does she
know about it, except the lies that she has been taught by demons
and evil angels? True, even with the Word of God in our hands,
we know only "in part"; but, thank God, a time is coming when
we shall know in whole, when "that which is perfect is come".

The resurrection *from* the dead

The Resurrection of the Body   14

The resurrection *from* the dead

The great fact of the resurrection of the dead was known all along the ages, and it was the hope of God's people; but a great secret was made known with regard to it by Jehovah to the Apostle Paul. Our Lord had previously given a hint of it when, coming down from the mountain of transfiguration (see the 9th chapter of Mark), he said that they should tell no man of the things they had seen until the Son of man were risen "from" the dead.

The disciples would not have been puzzled if the Lord had spoken simply of resurrection. He had merely spoken of resurrection, when He told Martha that her brother should rise again. She said, "I know that he shall rise again". But here He spoke of a different thing. He said here, "Till the Son of man be risen *from* the dead", and it says that they kept that saying to themselves, questioning one with another what the rising *from* the dead should mean.

The resurrection *of* the dead—of dead people—that they knew. As to this resurrection *from among* the dead, they wondered what it could mean. But the revelation was made to the Apostle Paul, and he writes in 1 Corinthians 15:51, "Behold, I show you a mystery"; that is, "Behold, I tell you a secret. I am going to tell you something that has hitherto remained hidden and been kept secret", just as the secret with regard to the Church—the Body of Christ—had been kept. "Behold, I tell you a secret. We shall not all sleep." And the heathen world before, and the world today who are ignorant of this secret, say one to another, "Ah, there are many things that are uncertain, but there is one thing that is certain, we must all die!" Thank God, we know a secret about

The Resurrection of the Body   15

that. We shall not all die; but whether we are alive and remain, or whether we fall asleep, we know that we shall be changed and raised at His coming.

I ought to remark, in passing, that wherever the resurrection of the Lord Jesus Christ is spoken of, and wherever the resurrection of His people is spoken of, it is always with this preposition, *"From among* the dead"*. It is not always observed in the *KJV*, but I believe that in the *RV* it is uniformly rendered *"from"*; so that, in studying this subject for yourselves, if you take the *RV* you will make no mistake about the true usage of the reference in this matter of the resurrection.

How are the dead raised?

How are the dead raised?

1. The Germ Theory

But now it is time for us to ask, "How are the dead raised up?" Of course, man has got his thoughts upon it, many thoughts; and of one thing we are perfectly sure, that we shall find that they are contrary to God's thoughts. We may summarize the whole of them in four great classes. We may call the *first* one the **germ** theory. It is a very ancient theory. It is an ancient Jewish theory. At any rate, it is a theory of the Talmud. It was entertained by some of the Fathers, such as Tertullian and Gregory of Nyssa and Basil. They supposed that there is a bone, or a certain substance, in the human body which nothing can destroy, and they say the name of it is "luz". You may pulverize it in a mortar, but you cannot destroy it. You cannot dissolve it in acids, or in other substances, and nothing upon earth can destroy it; and that is the germ from which the resurrection body will be made.

Well, after all, that is only an hypothesis. There is no Scripture for that at any rate, and what saith Scripture? It distinctly says, "That which thou sowest is not quickened except it die"; but this germ never dies, and therefore it cannot be quickened. "It is sown a natural body; it is raised a spiritual body." "That which is born of the flesh [and this germ is flesh] is flesh." The seed which is spoken of by the Holy Ghost in 1 Corinthians 15 is only an illustration. I think we can hardly say that it is intended to be an exactly analogous identical process; but it is an illustration, just as when the Lord said with regard to Himself, "Except a corn of wheat fall into the ground and die [and that means to dissolve and to go to corruption] it abideth alone; but if it die it bringeth forth much fruit". He referred to His own body. His own body did not die in that sense. It saw no corruption. And therefore the "much fruit" which it has produced shows that this is only an illustration.

2. The Identity Theory

And then the *second* great class of ideas may be included under the term of the **identity** theory. This is a later theory, but it was an early Christian theory, and several of the Fathers professed it. Tatian and Tertullian and others believed that cripples would rise cripples, that infants would rise infants. Jerome believed that everyone would rise at about thirty years of age, at whatever age he died. Of course, that is only theory. The Mahometans hold this; and the mediaeval or scholastic Fathers held that as a person died so he would be raised. That is why, at this very moment, if a Mahometan is wounded in battle, he will never suffer his limb to be amputated. He would rather die in any agony, because he believes that he will rise again exactly as he dies. But this theory is met by such scriptures as these: "Thou sowest not that body that shall be"; "Flesh and blood cannot inherit the kingdom of God." We know that the earthly house of this tabernacle is to be dissolved, and that we are to have a new house, a house from heaven. These scriptures effectually dispose of what we may call the identity theory.

3. The Re-incarnation Theory

And then the *third* theory we may call the **re-incarnation** theory. That is the theory of the great ancient religions of the East. It is being revived to-day under the guise of theosophy. Re-incarnation is one of the cardinal features of theosophy, the teaching of evil angels at the present moment. Satan is getting a circulation for this lie now, in order to prepare for the moment when he is to reincarnate the man of sin.

And there are many Christian writers who verge very closely on this theory. Even Archbishop Whately did in his *Future State*. There is something akin to it in Bishop Westcott's writings and in Bishop Perowne's. They illustrate it thus, that it is all the same if the spirit inhabits another body; it is only another house. You may take this house down, and you may build another house with the same material, and it is practically the same house. But it is *not* the same thing. The body is a *home* for us, and if the house of our childhood were taken down and another house were built, we should go to it and should want to find the room where we found the Saviour. We should want to find the room where our mother died, or where some holy and hallowed scene took place. No; it says, "We are *at home* in the body"; and Job says, "I shall see Him for *myself. Mine eyes* shall behold Him, even though my reins be consumed within me". The Scriptures always assume that it is *ourselves;* and that has led to what we have called the identity theory.

You remember the words of the Lord Jesus which we have just repeated, "I will raise it up again", "I will raise him up again", four times in John 6. Then the apostle says to the Thessalonian saints, "I pray God your whole spirit and soul and body be preserved blameless unto the coming of our Lord Jesus Christ". "Who shall change our vile bodies"—the bodies of our humiliation, our humble bodies—"and make them like His own body of glory". "We shall be changed." We ourselves shall be changed. "He that raised up Christ from the dead shall also quicken your mortal bodies by His Spirit that dwelleth in you". The law of continuity is utterly broken down by this theory of re-incarnation.

4. The Spiritual Body Theory

And then, *fourthly,* there is what we may call the **spiritual body** theory. It is the Swedenborgian theory; it is the theory of the spiritualists, the teaching of demons. It is much more popular than you imagine. But this is also an ancient error, and it leads, as it did lead, to the denial of the resurrection altogether.

According to this theory, resurrection practically takes place at death by a spiritual body which is evolved from the mortal body. However, this *utterly destroys resurrection as a hope;* because the hope which is held out to us is that those who are Christ's will be all raised together at His coming; not merely that we which are alive and remain are to be transformed together, but that those who are asleep are to be first raised, and then caught up together with the living ones to meet Him in the air. We are to be raised in a definite order:

> *Christ* the firstfruits; afterward they that are Christ's at His coming. (1 Corinthians 15:23,24)

We are to be raised at a definite *time*: at the appearing of the Lord Jesus Christ. The day of resurrection for the believer is not the hour of each believer's death, but it is the hour of the Lord's appearing. We are distinctly told by a direct revelation from the Lord, in 1 Thessalonians 4:15 (*RV*),

> That we that are alive, that are left unto the coming of the Lord, shall in no wise PRECEDE them that are fallen asleep.

Why shall we not precede them, or get before them? Why? Because they are to be raised first; and then, when they are raised and changed, we shall be changed and caught up together with them in the clouds, to meet the Lord in the air. It cannot be that *they* have so preceded *us!* But this spiritual body theory utterly and entirely destroys this blessed hope of resurrection *as a hope.* It utterly reverses the teaching of Scripture as to death and as to judgment. It makes a mockery of those two great solemn statements, "Thou shalt surely die", and, "There shall be no more death".

The Resurrection Body

The Resurrection Body

And what utterly negates this spiritual body theory is that the resurrection body is to be like Christ's, and we know that His body was not such a body. His was a glorious body, and His body is the very type and the likeness and the illustration and the definition of what the raised bodies of the saints are to be. "We know", in spite of all these hypotheses and thoughts and imaginations, "that when He shall appear we shall be *like Him*". How do we know it? Because God has told us that we shall be like Him. And what was He like? What was His resurrection body like? Well, as He came from the sepulchre the women held Him. So it was a body that could be held. He said to them, "Handle me, and see". So it was a body which could be handled, and a body which could be seen.

He said to Thomas, "Reach hither thy finger, and behold My hands: and reach hither thy hand, and thrust it into My side". So that it could be seen and handled and touched. The spear marks were visible, the prints of the nails must have been visible. And there is great meaning in those solemn words which refer to Israel, and yet await their fulfilment—"They shall look upon Me whom they have pierced".

We may imagine for a moment that solemn supper scene at Emmaus, when they knew not who He was; how when He blessed the bread, and lifted up His hands in blessing, they may have seen the marks of the nails.

He is the firstborn from the dead. He will have many brethren. It was by a resurrection of the dead that He was declared to be the Son of God (Romans 1:4). And that is how *we* shall be *declared to be the sons of God*. We have the blessed and high and holy privilege now; but it has to be "declared", it has to be "manifested", and we are told in Romans 8:19 when that manifestation will take place. It will be when the body shall be redeemed from the grave, and the manifestation of the sons of God shall take place at the coming of our Lord Jesus Christ in the air. Resurrection was His right, because He was Who He was. It is our blessed privilege and hope, because we are ***Whose*** *we are.*

How are the dead raised up?

How are the dead raised up?

Again we may ask, "How are the dead raised up?" And the answer to the question is, "By the power of God". Nicodemus asked, "How can these things be?" What was the answer? "God so loved the world, that He *gave* His only begotten Son". God's gift, therefore, was the answer to Nicodemus's "How?"

And so in the next chapter, when the woman of Samaria asked, "How is it that Thou, being a Jew, askest drink of me, which am a woman of Samaria?" Jesus said, "If thou knewest the Gift of God, and who it is that saith to thee, Give Me to drink, thou wouldest have asked of Him, and He would have given thee living water".

And so it is in 1 Corinthians 15:35. "But some man will say", says the apostle, "How are the dead raised up? And with what body do they come?" What is the answer? "God *giveth* it a body as it hath pleased Him" *(v 38)*.

The Gift
of God

The Gift of God

The gift of God, the power of God as manifested in the gift of God, is the only answer to all our questions; and, thank God, we know this. "We know", as it says in 2 Corinthians 5:1, "that if our earthly house of this tabernacle were dissolved". We know that *"If* it shall be dissolved". The particular Greek word for "if" there, with the mood of the verb that follows it, show that it is not at all a certainty. "If the house of our earthly tabernacle be dissolved." It is not at all certain that it will be. It may be. Of course, if we fall asleep in Jesus, it must be. But it may not be, because we may be "alive and remain" at His appearing. But, supposing that it should be dissolved, then we know that we have a better one. We know that we have a house that God Himself shall build. We know that we have no longer an earthly house, but a heavenly one. And when shall we have it? Many commentators—in fact, all that I have looked at—say that we have this at death. But you notice that this chapter begins with the word "For"; and it is one in a series of reasons for a statement that has been previously made in the 14th verse of the 4th chapter:

> Knowing that He which raised up the Lord Jesus shall raise up us also by Jesus, and shall present us with you.

How do we know it? By the next verse. *"For* all things", etc.; the next, *"For* which cause", etc.; the next, *"For* our light affliction", etc.; and then the verse of the next chapter, *"For* we know", etc. This is another of the reasons how it is that the Spirit which raised up the Lord Jesus shall raise us up and present us with Him. How? *"For* we know that if our earthly house of this tabernacle were dissolved, we have a building of God."

Transformation

Transformation

And that is how we shall be raised up, and that is how we shall be presented. It is no mere transition, it is no mere evolution; but it is a *transformation,* it is a manifestation, it is a transfiguration, it is a resurrection, it is "the redemption of our body" (Romans 8:23), it is the manifestation of our sonship. The Greek does not say "waiting for the adoption", but *waiting for the sonship,* waiting for the manifestation of our sonship in the resurrection of our bodies. So, while identity is not the word, **continuity** is the word, which really expresses the truth as to the transformation of God's people.

The bodies that we possess at this moment are the same bodies in one sense as when we were children. We have photographs of ourselves, doubtless, at different ages; one taken in infancy, another in childhood, another in youth, and now those that have been recently taken. It is the same body, and yet philosophically and scientifically it is not the same. It is all the same for us, at any rate. "He that was dead came forth." Lazarus it was who came forth, and not another. "He that was dead sat up, and began to speak", and not another. "Women received their dead raised to life again", and they knew them and spoke to them. The grave, thank God, has already been robbed of some of its prey, and there are those who are to escape death altogether. The grave has been robbed of many, and death has been baffled by two [Christ and Lazarus]; and, if we may answer this question, "How are the dead raised up?" in a definite statement, I would express it by the words *continuity* and re-creation: and that is why we are exhorted in 1 Peter 4:19,

> Wherefore let them that suffer according to the will of God commit the keeping of their souls to Him in well

doing, as unto a faithful Creator.

In fact, the transfiguration of the Lord Jesus Christ Himself is the type of the resurrection body, and that was a visible body. Moses and Elijah "appeared in glory", it says. But Christ's body was so glorious, and His raiment so white, "as no fuller on earth can white them". It was the glory of the revelation of the King. It is a specimen of the King coming in His kingdom with those who had been raised from the dead and those who had been changed.

A New Creation

A New Creation

But let us for a moment pay a visit, as Jeremiah did, to the potter's house, in Jeremiah 18:1-4.

> The word which came to Jeremiah from the Lord, saying, Arise, and go down to the potter's house, and there I will cause thee to hear My words. Then I went down to the potter's house, and, behold, he wrought a work on the wheels. And the vessel that he made of clay was marred in the hand of the potter: so he made it again another vessel, as seemed good to the potter to make it. (In the margin we read "he returned and made".)

If we look at the immediate context, we will find that the *interpretation* of these words refers to the house of Israel; but there is an *application* of the words that goes very much farther than their interpretation. The context shows that the *interpretation* belongs solely to the house of Israel; but we may *apply* the passage as exhibiting a great and divine principle which we see in all the works of God.

You see it, for example, in the *covenant* of works which He made with Israel. That was made, and man has always marred everything with which God has ever entrusted him. "Which My covenant they brake". The first covenant of works was like that vessel marred upon the wheels; and then He made another as seemed good to the potter to make it. And it is written of this covenant that if the first "had been faultless, then should no place have been sought for the second" (Hebrews 8:7); but it was broken by His *faulty people,* and therefore a new covenant was made as it pleased the potter to make it.

And so it is with regard to *the earth*. The earth was created in glory and beauty, but it has been marred. Sin entered, the curse was pronounced, and this earth has been marred in the hands of the potter. It is not going to be mended, but there is going to be a new one.

> "I saw a new heaven and a new earth: for the first heaven and the first earth were passed away." (Revelation 21:1)

And it was made "as it seemed good to the potter to make it".

It is true of our *old nature* that it has been marred in our first parents, and we know how it is marred in each one of us. It is never God's principle to mend that which man has marred. He always makes something new. And so He now makes a new creation in Christ Jesus. As the old nature is fallen and marred, man must have a new nature given to him. The new wine cannot be put into old wine skins, the new piece of cloth cannot be put upon the old garment; but the new wine must be put into new wine skins, and then both are preserved.

Transformed Bodies

Transformed bodies

And so with our bodies. These *bodies* of humiliation, which are made of clay like the vessel of the potter, have been marred upon the wheel. As soon as we are born we begin to die. There are the seeds of suffering and disease and death in every one of us. We are made of clay, and marred upon the wheel. But the potter "returned" and made it again another vessel, as it seemed good to the potter to make it.

And so with these transformed bodies at the resurrection, when the great potter Himself shall return. He will make them again another body, as it hath pleased Him: and so, whether it be the old nature, whether it be the heart, whether it be our bodies, they are never mended or repaired or improved or reformed; but they are condemned, and a new nature and a new heart is given, and by-and-by new bodies will be bestowed. Oh, what a depth of meaning there is in those few simple words—"He made it again another vessel, as seemed good to the potter to make it". "God giveth it a body as it hath pleased Him" (1 Corinthians 15:38).

New glorious bodies

New glorious bodies

And so you find in Hebrews 10, with reference to the sacrifices and offerings which were under the first covenant, it is said they are all taken away because they were marred in their use; and then He said, "Lo, I come to do Thy will, O God". In each case:

> "He taketh away the first, that He may establish the second". (Hebrews 10:9)

Thank God, *the second is always established.* And so it will be with these new glorious bodies. They will be established. These poor vile bodies will be soon taken away and disestablished; but that which is to come will be established for ever and ever in glory.

That Blessed Hope

That Blessed Hope

This is our hope, and you will see how it is all bound up in Christ. It shuts us up entirely to Him; but people do not heed it. The shepherds went and told the people about His *first coming*. It says, the people "wondered". That is all. The people wondered, and they went on talking about the topics of the day. The topics of the day were very much like the topics of our day—taxes, and commerce, and politics. Augustus had just made a taxing throughout the empire, and that was doubtless the great matter of conversation. They "wondered", and passed on with their business.

But the early Christians cherished this blessed hope, and the testimony of Gibbon is worth repeating. It is contained in a few words from the 15th chapter of his 1st volume. This great truth of the Lord's coming, and our being raised at His coming, was universally believed among these early Christians. He says,

> "The approach of this event had been predicted by the apostles. The tradition of it was preserved by their nearest disciples, and those who understood in their literal sense the discourses of Christ Himself were obliged to expect the coming of the Son of man before that generation was totally extinguished." [That is where Gibbon was wrong. They were not *obliged* to expect it before that generation was extinguished; but the fact remains that they did.] "As long as for wise purposes this error" [you see we have the testimony of *an enemy* who does not believe this truth himself] "as long as for wise purposes this error was permitted to subsist in the church, *it was productive of the most salutary effect on the faith and practice of Christians*."

The Resurrection of the Body   55

There is the testimony of an enemy then to this truth, as to the effect it produced upon the lives of those who held it. Oh, that Christians today would try this experiment! Oh, that we might be influenced by this blessed hope now! That we might accustom ourselves to looking for it, just as an army is practised in meeting a night attack, or just as upon a vessel the crew is practised by a false alarm of fire, so that each man may go to his right station.

Oh that we might rehearse for ourselves, and practice for ourselves, the waiting for this assembling shout— the waiting to hear the voice of the archangel and the trump of God! That will be an assembling shout. The trump of God is for the same purpose. See in Numbers 10:7, "When the congregation is *to be gathered together*, ye shall blow". And when His people are to be gathered together in the air this trump of God shall sound. But He says, "Ye shall not sound *an alarm*". No, it will be the signal for our being gathered together unto Him. It will not be an alarm for us, but it will be a blessed assembling shout and gathering trump.

Our walk today and the future hope of being like Christ

Our walk today and the future hope of being like Christ

As Christ is the blessed object and centre of our hope, so He is presented to us in this great subject. "He that hath this hope in Him"—not in himself—"He that hath this hope in Christ". What hope? Why the hope of being like Him at His appearing, when we shall see Him as He is. He that hath this hope fixed upon Him, what does he do? What is the effect of it? "Every one that hath this hope in Him purifieth himself, even as He is pure." Yes, it *is a purifying hope.*

And why is the low standard of walk among Christians at the present day so much deplored? Why are so many efforts put forth for raising the standard of this walk? *Because that standard has been changed!* And why? Because this purifying hope is not held.

Why are other methods tried and sought after for the promotion of purity of life, and this great divine *advent method* not tried? Here is God's method to secure our purity of life and walk. "He that hath this hope" (of the transformation of His people)—he that hath this blessed hope fixed upon him—"purifieth himself". And this Divine method cannot be carried too far.

Other methods which men may propose to you may be carried too far. They *are* carried too far; but you will never carry this one too far. You can never look *to* Christ too much. You can never look *for* Christ too much. There will never be any ill effect from looking to Him; and, whatever may be left uncertain from the

The Resurrection of the Body   59

consideration of this subject, we may be sure that, with all our knowledge and all our thoughts about it, we shall surely say, when this blessed hope is realized, "The half was not told me". It will surely be beyond all that we have ever expected: it will surely exceed all that we ever desired: for "it doth not yet appear what we shall be: but we know that, when He shall appear, we shall be like Him; for we shall see Him as He is".

About the Author

Ethelbert W. Bullinger D.D. (1837-1913) was a direct descendent of Heinrich Bullinger, the great Swiss reformer who carried on Zwingli's work after the latter had been killed in war.

E. W. Bullinger was brought up a Methodist but sang in the choir of Canterbury Cathedral in Kent. He trained for and became an Anglican minister before becoming Secretary of the Trinitarian Bible Society. He was a man of intense spirituality and made a number of outstanding contributions to biblical scholarship and broad-based evangelical Christianity.

This book originally appeared as three articles in *Things to Come* in about 1905. It has been reprinted here from those articles without change. I have left the text the same, except for sub-headings which have been put in to break up the continuous text and, hopefully, to help the reader follow the argument.

Thus this booklet includes the view Bullinger held *at the time he wrote* on the hope of the Church which is the Body of Christ; namely that it was "to meet the Lord in the air". Bullinger was later to change that view and concluded that the hope of this Church, spoken of in Ephesians and Colossians, should be distinguished from the hope of the Acts period, during which 1 Thessalonians 4 was written. Thus the "meeting the Lord in the air" was replaced by looking for Christ's "appearing in glory".

These later views were expressed in a series of Editorials under the heading "The Lord hath Spoken" which appeared in *Things to Come* from 1911 to 1913.

They were later published posthumously in his last book *The Foundations of Dispensational Truth*.

Michael Penny

Also by E W Bullinger

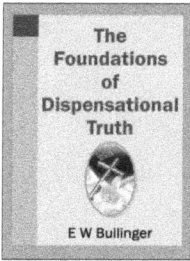

The Foundations of Dispensation Truth

Bullinger's last book, reflecting his mature views.

This is Bullinger's last book and is his definitive work on the subject of dispensationalism. It covers the ministries of ...

- the prophets,
- the Son of God,
- those that heard Christ, and
- the ministry of Paul, the Apostle to the Gentiles.

He comments on the Gospels and the Pauline epistles and has a lengthy section on the Acts of the Apostles, followed by one explaining why miraculous signs of the Acts period ceased.

This is a newly typeset book, well presented in an easy to read format.

Copies of this book are available from www.obt.org.uk and from
The Open Bible Trust,
Fordland Mount, Upper Basildon, Reading, RG8 8LU.

It is also available as an eBook from Amazon Kindle and Apple.

**The following is a selection of works by E W Bullinger
Published by The Open Bible Trust**

The Transfiguration
The Knowledge of God
God's Purpose in Israel
The Prayers of Ephesians
The Lord's Day (Revelation 1:10)
The Rich Man and Lazarus
The Importance of Accuracy
Christ's Prophetic Teaching
The Resurrection of the Body
The Divine Names and Titles
The Spirits in Prison: 1 Peter 3:17-4:6
The Lesson of the Book of Job: The Oldest Lesson in the World
The Seven Sayings to the Woman at the Well
The Foundations of Dispensational Truth
The Christian's Greatest Need
Introducing the Church Epistles
The Two Natures in the Child of God
The Name of Jehovah in the Book of Esther
The Names and Order of the Books of the Old Testament
The Second Advent in Relation to the Jew
The Vision of Isaiah: Its Structure and Scope
The Importance of Accuracy: in the study of the Bible

**More information about the above can be seen on
www.obt.org.uk
from where they can be ordered.**

They are also available as eBooks
from Amazon Kindle and Apple.

Further Reading on Resurrection

If you have benefited from this study on resurrection, then you will find *Resurrection! When?* by Sylvia and Michael Penny of interest. It deals with such issues as "Will Christians be resurrected *before* Christ's return?" before going on to consider such issues as the *first* resurrection, the *second* resurrection, a *better* resurrection, and the judgment of the *living* at Christ's return.

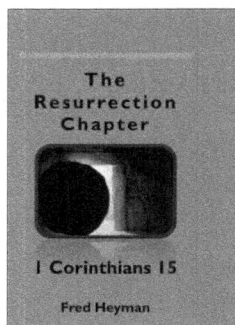

Resurrection! When
By Michael and Sylvia Penny

If there is no resurrection of the dead … What then?
By Charles Ozanne

The Resurrection Chapter: 1 Corinthians 15
By Fred Heyman

Further details of these can be seen on www.obt.org.uk from where copies can be ordered.

They are also available as eBooks from Amazon and Apple.

Further Reading

Approaching the Bible

by Michael Penny

A good book for those who want to study seriously the Word of God. It delves into the basic areas to lay a good foundation for understanding the message using certain guidelines set by Miles Coverdale.
(Reviewed by Frank Wren in *The Trumpet Sounds*, GB)

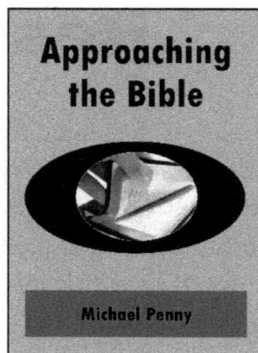

This is a thoroughgoing exposition and defence of the dispensational approach to interpreting the Bible. The author traces what he believes to be such an approach from some of the earliest Church Fathers onwards, points out the strengths and weaknesses in the dispensational system of modern interpreters, and advocates what he holds to be an improved approach.
(Reviewed by Paul C. Clark in *Librarian's World*, USA)

This is a book of sterling quality, a much needed introduction to dispensational truth, simple and lucid, but at the same time comprehensive and profound ... Dispensational truth comes across, not as a fad of certain extremists, but as a natural and inevitable result of a normal, natural and plain reading of the Bible ... A book we can without hesitation pass on or recommend to any who may inquire about our beliefs."
(Reviewed by Charles Ozanne in *Search*, GB)

40 Problem Passages

Michael Penny

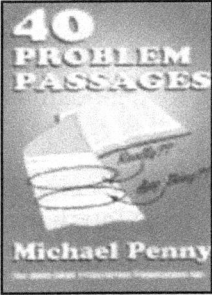

This book is a sequel to the author's earlier book *Approaching the Bible* It applies the principles set out there to *40 Problem Passages* from the Bible. In other words, it follows the advice given by Miles Coverdale. That advice was based on asking such questions as:

- "Who" were these words written to, or "Who" were they about?
- "Where" is this to take place?
- "When" was it written or "When" is it about?
- "What", precisely, is said?
- "Why" did God say it, do it, or will do it?

After asking such questions, we then will have a better understanding of the Bible and can "apply" that passage to our lives today.

There are far more that *40 Problem Passages* in the Bible! However, in this book the author not only solves these *40 Problem Passages*, he also equips the reader with a method by which many, many more problem passages can be understood.

Please **visit www.obt.org.uk** for more information on this book, including a list of the 40 passages considered.

Copies can be ordered from that website or from
The Open Bible Trust
Fordland Mount, Upper Basildon, Reading, RG8 8LU, UK.

It is also available as an eBook from Amazon Kindle and Apple.

Think on These Things

by Ernest Streets

This volume constitutes the collected writings of Ernest Streets who was pastor of Cowdenbeath Gospel Mission in Scotland for 63 years. Concentrated in these pages is a wealth of wisdom and careful Bible study. Most Christians have learnt the truth at second hand from the writings of others, but Mr. Streets discovered it for himself, solely from reading the Bible and waiting on the Lord. In this volume will be found many insights into the meaning of the Bible, insights which are bound to cause the reader to *think on these things*, however much or little he may know already. The subjects covered include:

- Think on These Things
- Paul's Ministry
- The Gospel of your Salvation (Ephesians 1:13)
- The Eternal Purpose in Christ Jesus our Lord (Ephesians 3:11)
- The Mystery of the Gospel of God (Ephesians 6:19)
- The Body of Christ (Ephesians 4:12)
- Do you understand what you are Reading?
- These signs
- To the Jew first
- Scriptural proof of the "living hope"
- The Last Twelve Verses of Mark's Gospel
- The Covenants
- The Lord's Table
- Another Look at the Gospel of John

The Church! When did it begin?
(And why is that important?)
by Olive and Lloyd Allen

I cannot speak too highly of this book. In my view it is the best statement of beliefs regarding dispensational truth that has yet been written. The whole subject is discussed fully and fairly. It is presented only as a 'personal opinion offered for consideration only'. But the reader is inexorably carried along by the easy conversational style to arrive at the same conclusion as the writers. The book is in two parts.

- Part 1 seeks to answer the question, "When did the Church begin?"
- Part 2 considers the question, "Why does it matter when the Church began?"

The writers wisely start off by stating basic principles and defining key words. No honest, open-minded believer can fail to be impressed by this carefully-argued and well written work.

(Review by Charles Ozanne in *Search*, UK)

**The Open Bible Trust
Fordland Mount, Upper Basildon,
Reading, RG8 8LU, UK**

Free Magazine

About this Book

The Resurrection of the Body

Each Easter time Christians celebrate the resurrection from the dead of our Lord Jesus Christ, but the Bible has a lot to say about the resurrection of each Christian; that is, the resurrection of the body. In fact it is the hope of each and every believer in Jesus Christ. As Paul wrote in Philippians 3:20-21:

> But our citizenship is in heaven. And we eagerly await a Saviour from there, the Lord Jesus Christ, who, by the power that enables him to bring everything under his control, will transform our lowly bodies so that they will be like his glorious body.

That being the case, what does the Bible say about *The Resurrection of the Body*? In this book Bullinger answers that question.

Publications of The Open Bible Trust must be in accordance with its evangelical, fundamental and dispensational basis. However, beyond this minimum, writers are free to express whatever beliefs they may have as their own understanding, provided that the aim in so doing is to further the object of The Open Bible Trust. A copy of the doctrinal basis is available on **www.obt.org.uk** or from:

THE OPEN BIBLE TRUST
Fordland Mount, Upper Basildon
Reading, RG8 8LU, GB